The Revolutionary War

Researching American History

introduced and edited by

Pat Perrin

Army camp at Valley Forge, winter of 1777-1778. Eleven thousand men braved the cold and snow at the camp, 20 miles northwest of Philadelphia.

Discovery Enterprises, Ltd.
Carlisle, Massachusetts

First Edition © Discovery Enterprises, Ltd., Carlisle, MA 2000

ISBN 1-57960-061-1

Library of Congress Catalog Card Number 00-103461

10 9 8 7 6 5 4 3 2

Printed in the United States of America

Subject Reference Guide:

Title: *The Revolutionary War*
Series*: Researching American History*
introduced and edited by Pat Perrin

Nonfiction
Analyzing documents re: Revolutionary War

Credits:

Cover illustration:
Darley's drawing of a minuteman, preparing for battle.
All illustrations are from John Grafton, ed., *The American Revolution – A Picture Sourcebook*. New York: Dover Publications, Inc., 1975, except as otherwise noted in the text.

An especially useful source was the History Place website, at:
http://www.historyplace.com/united states/revoluton

Acknowledgments:

Special thanks to Jeanne Munn Bracken, editor of
The Shot Heard 'Round the World: The Beginnings of the American Revolution and *Women in the American Revolution,* both published by Discovery Enterprises, Ltd, for her research which added greatly to this book.

Contents

About the Series

Researching American History is a series of books which introduces various topics and periods in our nation's history through the study of primary source documents.

Reading the Historical Documents

On the following pages you'll find words written by people during or soon after the time of the events. This is firsthand information about what life was like back then. Illustrations are also created to record history. These historical documents are called **primary source materials**.

At first, some things written in earlier times may seem difficult to understand. Language changes over the years, and the objects and activities described might be unfamiliar. Also, spellings were sometimes different. Below is a model which describes how we help with these challenges.

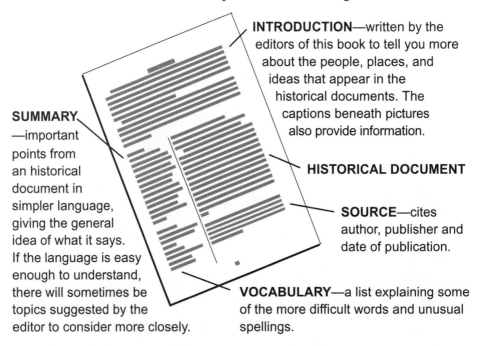

INTRODUCTION—written by the editors of this book to tell you more about the people, places, and ideas that appear in the historical documents. The captions beneath pictures also provide information.

SUMMARY—important points from an historical document in simpler language, giving the general idea of what it says. If the language is easy enough to understand, there will sometimes be topics suggested by the editor to consider more closely.

HISTORICAL DOCUMENT

SOURCE—cites author, publisher and date of publication.

VOCABULARY—a list explaining some of the more difficult words and unusual spellings.

In these historical documents, you may see three periods (…) called an ellipsis. It means that the editor has left out some words or sentences. You may see some words in brackets, such as [and]. These are words the editor has added to make the meaning clearer. When you use a document in a paper you're writing, you should include any ellipses and brackets it contains, just as you see them here. Be sure to give complete information about the author, title, and publisher of anything that was written by someone other than you.

Introduction:
Having a Revolution

by Pat Perrin

A Revolution is an effort to change old ways of seeing and doing things. When more and more people become discontented, sometimes the force for change becomes too great to stop. If the revolution succeeds, it dramatically alters a country from the inside.

The American Revolution—or Revolutionary War—lasted from 1775-1783. You can use the table of contents of this book as a timeline to follow the action. This revolution was a rebellion by the 13 British colonies in America against Great Britain. A **colony** is a territory settled by a group of people from another land. It's still ruled by the land that the people came from.

Great Britain includes England, Scotland, and Wales. **England** is the largest part, and people from there are referred to as English or as British. At the time of the American Revolution, the King of England was George III.

Parliament makes the laws in Great Britain. After 1688, Parliament was more powerful than the monarch (king or queen). American colonists deeply resented not having any vote in Parliament. It meant they had no control over their own laws.

Political parties in England included the Whigs and Tories. The **Tories** supported the monarch and generally resisted change. In the colonies, those who wanted to remain part of Great Britain called themselves **Loyalists**. Rebelling colonists often called them Tories, after the party in England.

The settlers who thought the colonies should be independent called themselves **Patriots**. (A patriot is someone who loves, supports, and defends his or her country.) The British called them **Rebels**.

By 1775, there were 2,225,000 settlers in the American colonies, which were scattered through a huge wilderness. Ways of life varied greatly from one colony to another. Some colonies thought of themselves almost as separate countries. Aside from the English-speaking colonists, there were many from other European countries. And there were also slaves—especially in the southern colonies—most of whom had been brought from Africa.

About 60,000 Loyalists lived in the colonies, mostly along the coast. Even after the revolution started, the British believed that Loyalists could soon take control of the colonies. When the Patriots won, the American colonies became independent of Great Britain. The 13 colonies became 13 states. They formed the United States of America.

Detail from "The Cruel Massacre of the Protestants, in North America Shewing how the French and Indians join together to scalp the English." London, about 1760. (From The French and Indian War—an Album)

Years of Unrest

In 1763, most people in the British colonies referred to themselves as English or British. Sometimes they identified themselves by their colony—as Virginians, for example. Most of them thought the English system of government was the best in the world, but they did want a voice in it.

In Europe, many ideas were being discussed about the nature of human beings and how they ought to live. European ideas filtered into the colonies through the cities. Americans became convinced that they should be able to control their own lives.

Except for their slaves, the people in the colonies already had more freedom than most others of that time. The colonies had popularly elected houses of assembly. Through these, each colony had a great deal of control over its internal affairs.

The colonies weren't in the habit of cooperating with each other very much—at least, not until they felt that they had a common problem. They all had their own claims to boundaries and to western land. But after a series of problems with England, the colonists finally got annoyed enough to begin to work together.

1755-1763—An Expensive War

Europeans from several different countries came to explore and live in the New World. The British brought their families with them and built colonies along the eastern coast. In the Northeast, French fur traders and missionaries often lived among the Native Americans.

British settlers and French traders argued over land and fought for control of the waterways. After years of small battles and raids, war was declared in 1755. We call the conflict the French and Indian War; in Europe it's called the Seven Years War. It was mostly fought in what is now eastern Canada and the northeastern United States.

Most Native American nations sided with the French. Except for the Iroquois—who had never forgiven the French for demonstrating the gun by killing several braves.

The British surrounded the important French city of Quebec, but couldn't take it. In September, British troops again lined up outside the city. Their leader was General Wolfe. As they waited for the French to attack, Wolfe spoke to his troops.

General Wolfe To His Army

This day puts it into your power to terminate [this long]… Siege. Possessed with full confidence of the certain success which British valour must gain over such enemies, I have led you up to these steep and dengerous rocks…to shew you the foe within your reach. The impossibility of a retreat makes no difference in the situation of men resolved to conquer or die: and, believe me, my friends if your conquest could be bought with the blood of your general, he would most cheerfully resign a life which he has long devoted to his country.

Source: Captain John Knox, *Historical Journal of the Campaigns in North America For the Years 1757, 1758, 1759, and 1760.* Toronto: The Champlain Society, 1916, p. 335.

Summary:

Today you can end this long siege. British courage always wins. I show you the enemy, within your reach. Retreat is impossible. That doesn't matter when men decide to win or die. If my death could buy your victory, I would cheerfully give up my life. It has always been devoted to my country.

Vocabulary:

dengerous = dangerous
possessed with = having
shew = show
siege = blockade
terminate = end
valour = courage

Wolfe's words were prophetic (a good prediction of the future). Wolfe did die in the battle for Quebec, and the British did win the battle.

The French leader at Quebec was the Marquis de Montcalm. He also turned out to be good at predicting the future.

Summary:

If Wolfe beats me here, France has completely lost America. Then, 10 years later, America will revolt against England.

Vocabulary:

conclusion = opinion

utterly = completely

Statement by the Marquis de Montcalm

"If [Woolfe] beats me here, France has lost America utterly: yes, and one's only conclusion is, in ten years farther, America will be in revolt against England!"

Source: "The Marquis de Montcalm, August 24, 1759." Found in Flowler Barney, *The Adirondack Album,* Volume Two, New York, 1980, p. 29.

When the French and Indian War ended in 1763, Britain had won all the land east of the Mississippi River, except Louisiana. But it had been a very expensive war. The British had built forts along the frontier. Now they decided to keep their soldiers in America, rather than bring them home.

A lot of money had been spent to protect the colonies. So—reasoned the British—the colonies should help pay the bills. The British put higher taxes, or customs fees, on goods imported from England. Although they were prosperous, the colonists resented those new charges. After all, they had been given no vote in the matter.

1768-1772—Trouble in Boston

Bostonians hated the new customs fees on imports. John Hancock was a wealthy shipper who would later sign the Declaration of Independence. In 1768, he refused to pay the taxes on his shipload of wine. Instead, someone locked up the customs officers and unloaded the wine illegally.

In 1770, the Boston Massacre occurred. A mob carrying stones and snowballs harassed British soldiers on patrol. Someone fired a shot! The soldiers fired into the crowd—killing five colonists. The soldiers were tried and found innocent of murder. Two were found guilty of manslaughter, branded, and released.

Colonist Sam Adams was active in Massachusetts government. In 1772, he called a Boston town meeting. That group insisted the colonies had the right to rule themselves.

Boston Tea Party, artist unknown (The American Revolution Picture Sourcebook, New York: Dover Publications, 1975, p. 10)

1773—The Boston Tea Party

The British juggled the rules for importing tea to favor their own East India Company. Angry Bostonian merchants protested. On December 16, 1773, they dressed up as Indians and raided three ships carrying tea. They dumped so much tea in the water that it made islands all over the harbor. One of the raiders was colonist George Hewes.

The Boston Tea Party
by George Hewes

...It was now evening, and I immediately dressed myself in the costume of an Indian, equipped with a small hatchet, which I and my associates denominated the tomahawk, and a club. After having painted my face and hands with coal dust in the shop of a blacksmith, I [went] to Griffin's wharf, where the ships lay that contained the tea.

...In about three hours from the time we went on board, we had...broken and thrown overboard every tea chest to be found on the ship....

Source: Jeanne Munn Bracken, ed., *The Shot Heard 'Round the World: The Beginnings of the American Revolution.* Carlisle, MA: Discovery Enterprises, Ltd., 1995, p. 13.

Summary:

That evening, I dressed as an Indian. I had a small hatchet, which we called a tomahawk, and a club. I painted my face and hands dark. We went to the wharf where the ships were that held the tea.

About three hours after we went on board, we had broken every tea chest on the ship. We had thrown them all overboard.

Vocabulary:
associates = partners
denominated = called

The Boston Tea Party was celebrated in this popular poem by an anonymous author. It compares England to a mother and the Colonies to her daughter.

Summary:

An old lady was queen of an island. Her daughter lived on the other side of the ocean. The old lady was rich, but was never happy with what she had. She wanted her daughter to pay a tax of three cents a pound on tea.

[In another verse, the daughter refuses, and the mother insists.]

So the old lady sent her daughter a large package of tea. She ordered her servant to bring home the tax. She said her daughter must obey or be whipped.

The tea was delivered, but the girl poured it into the water. "Mother," she said, "You can have your tea when it's ready to drink, but no tax from me."

Vocabulary:
conveyed = carried
pence = pennies
quoth = said
steeped = soaked in hot
  water

Revolutionary Tea

There was an old lady lived over the sea,
And she was an island queen;
Her daughter lived off in a new country,
With an ocean of water between.
The old lady's pockets were filled with gold,
But never contented was she,
So she called on her daughter to pay her a tax,
Of three pence a pound on the tea.
Of three pence a pound on the tea.

. . . .

And so the old lady her servant called up,
And packed off a package of tea,
And eager for three pence a pound, she put in
Enough for a large family.
She ordered her servant to bring home the tax,
Declaring her child should obey,
Or old as she was and a woman most grown,
She'd half whip her life away,
She'd half whip her life away.

The tea was conveyed to the daughter's door,
And all down by the ocean side,
And the bouncing girl poured out every pound,
In the dark and boiling tide,
And then she called out to the island queen,
"O mother, dear mother," quoth she,
"Your tea you may have when 'tis steeped
    enough,
But never a tax from me,
But never a tax from me."

Source: Wanda Willson Whitman, ed., *Songs that Changed the World*. New York: Crown, 1969, p. 2.

1774—Intolerable Acts and Approaching War

After the Boston Tea Party, the British made new laws for the American Colonies. One closed the Boston harbor until Massachusetts paid for the destroyed tea. The British took over all political power, forbidding town meetings held without permission. They extended the Canadian border into territory claimed by Massachusetts, Connecticut, and Virginia. And they said that colonists had to house and feed British soldiers.

The colonists called these and other new laws the Intolerable Acts. ("Intolerable" means "unbearable.") In response, they formed the First Continental Congress—a new governing body with representatives from all the colonies. Patrick Henry, George Washington, Sam Adams, and John Hancock were there. The Congress urged colonists to arm themselves and prepare to defend their right to "life, liberty, and property."

Afraid that the British might find and seize their hidden weapons and ammunition, the Patriots kept close watch on them.

Paul Revere's account of the Committee's secret meetings

...in the fall of 1774 and the winter of 1775, I was one of upwards of thirty...who formed ourselves into a Committee for the purpose of watching the Movements of the British Soldiers, and gaining every intelligence of the movements of the Tories. We held our meetings at the Green-Dragon tavern. We were so careful that our meetings should be kept secret, that every time we met, every person swore upon the Bible that they would not discover any of our transactions, but to Messrs. [John] Hancock ...and one or two more.

Source: Edmund S. Morgan, ed., *Paul Revere's Three Accounts of his Famous Ride.* Boston: A Revolutionary War Bicentennial Commission and Massachusetts Historical Society Publication, 1967.

Summary:

In the fall of 1774 and winter of 1775, more than 30 of us formed a group to watch the British soldiers. We got all the information we could about the Tories. We made everyone promise not to tell anyone except certain men.

Vocabulary:

discover = reveal
intelligence = knowledge
upwards of = more than

The Battles Begin

In February of 1775, Virginia colonist Patrick Henry spoke against British rule, saying "Give me liberty or give me death!" The British decided to clamp down on the colonists. They ordered the Massachusetts military governor, General Thomas Gage, to use force to bring things back under control.

April 1775—Paul Revere Rides

British troops were spotted on the march in Boston. Patriots lit signals in the church steeple, and sent out riders to warn two nearby Middlesex County towns. Weapons and gunpowder were hidden at Concord, and John Hancock and Sam Adams were hiding at Lexington.

Paul Revere was a Patriot. That spring, he rode up and down the countryside, taking messages to other colonists. He became the most famous of messengers when Longfellow's well-known poem was published in 1860.

Summary:

Listen to the story of Paul Revere's midnight ride. It was April 18, 1775. Hardly anyone is still living who can remember it.

Revere said, "Hang a lantern in the church tower as a signal. Put one if the British come by land, and two if they come by sea. I'll be on the other shore, ready to ride and tell everyone to arm themselves.

Vocabulary:

aloft = high up
belfry = bell tower or
    steeple
seventy-five = 1775

Paul Revere's Ride (an excerpt)
by Henry Wadsworth Longfellow

Listen, my children, and you shall hear
Of the midnight ride of Paul Revere,
On the eighteenth of April, in seventy-five;
Hardly a man is now alive
Who remembers that famous day and year.

. . . .

He said to his friend, "If the British march
By land or sea from the town to-night,
Hang a lantern aloft in the belfry arch
Of the North Church tower as a signal light,
One, if by land, and two, if by sea;
And I on the opposite shore will be,
Ready to ride and spread the alarm
Through every Middlesex village and farm,
For the country folk to be up and to arm."

Source: Henry Wadsworth Longfellow, *Tales of a Wayside Inn,* 1860.

Paul Revere's Ride, by Darley

Paul Revere's own account of his ride

....I set off upon a very good Horse; it was then about 11 o'Clock, and very pleasant. After I had passed Charlestown Neck...I saw two men on Horse back, under a Tree. When I got near them, I discovered they were British officers. One tryed to git a head of Me, and the other to take me. I turned my horse very quick, and Galloped towards Charlestown neck, and then pushed for the Medford Road. The one who chased me, endeavoring to Cut me off, got into a Clay pond...I got clear of him.... In Medford, I awaked the Captain of the Minute men; and after that, I alarmed almost every house, till I got to Lexington.... I likewise mentioned, that we had better allarm all the Inhabitents till we got to Concord.

Source: Edmund S. Morgan, ed., *Paul Revere's Three Accounts of His Famous Ride.* Boston: A Revolutionary War Bicentennial Commission and Massachusetts Historical Society Publication, 1967.

Summary:

I had a good horse. Two British officers tried to cut me off and catch me. I galloped back, then headed fast for Medford Road. One officer's horse got into mud. I got away. In Medford, I warned our soldiers, and everybody between there and Lexington. I said we'd better warn everyone on the way to Concord.

Vocabulary:
alarmed; allarm = warned; warn
endeavoring = trying
git = get
inhabitents = inhabitants; those who live there
tryed = tried

The action at Lexington, by Darley

April 1775—Lexington and Concord

In April 1775, General Gage sent British soldiers to seize gunpowder that the colonists had stored at Concord. However, Paul Revere and other riders had warned the Patriots that the soldiers were coming. As a result, the British troops only found part of the gunpowder that had been there.

Military units had been organized in Massachusetts that could be ready "at a minute's notice." They were called minutemen. On their way to Concord, the British met a local company of minutemen at Lexington, and killed several of them. Amos Barrett was a 23-year-old corporal of the Concord minutemen.

Summary:

We went to meet the British. When they got close, we marched in front of them, playing our drums and flutes. They were playing, too. We had great music.

Vocabulary:

fifes = flutes

rod = 5.5 yards

Amos Barrett's account of the minutemen

We thought we would go and meet the British. We marched down towards Lexington about a mile and a half, and we see them a-coming. We halted and stayed there until we got within about 100 rods, then we was ordered to about face and marched before them with our drums and fifes a-going and also the British. We had grand music.

Source: Jeanne Munn Bracken, ed., *The Shot Heard 'Round the World: The Beginnings of the American Revolution.* Carlisle, MA: Discovery Enterprises, Ltd., 1995, p 26.

On their way back to Boston, the British were constantly attacked by Massachusetts troops and other Patriots along the road. The British suffered 273 casualties. In Boston, they soon found themselves surrounded by colonial volunteers. The Patriots held Boston under siege for a year.

General Gage wrote back to England, warning his superiors that the American soldiers wouldn't be easy to beat. The British made the mistake of paying little attention to Gage's warnings.

General Thomas Gage's letter to England

They are now spirited up by a rage and enthusiasm as great as ever people were possessed of, and you must proceed in earnest or give the business up. A small body acting in one spot will not avail. You must have large armies, making diversions on different sides to divide their force.

The loss we have sustained is greater than we can bear. Small armies can't afford such losses.... The troops were sent out too late, the Rebels were at least two months [ahead of] us, and your Lordship would be astonished to see the tract of country they have entrenched and fortified; their number is great, so many hands have been employed....

...I have before wrote to your Lordship my opinion that a large army must at length be employed to reduce these people, and mentioned the hiring of foreign troops. I fear it must come to that, or else to avoid a land war and make use only of your fleet.

Source: Jeanne Munn Bracken, ed., *The Shot Heard 'Round the World: The Beginnings of the American Revolution*. Carlisle, MA: Discovery Enterprises, Ltd., 1995, pp. 35-6.

Summary:

They are as angry and eager as can be. You must take them seriously, or give it up. A small army in one place won't do. You need large armies on each side to divide them.

We have had greater losses than a small army can stand. Our troops were sent too late; the Rebels were two months ahead. You'd be amazed to see how much land they have dug into and fortified. There are so many of them. We may have to hire foreign troops or avoid land war and stick to naval battles.

Vocabulary:

in earnest = seriously
spirited up = eager
avail = help
diversions = distractions
sustained = borne; experienced
entrenched = dug in
fortified = built defenses for (such as walls)

The British were shocked! Untrained colonists had defeated the strongest army in the world. They had forgotten how many Patriots had fought against the French and Indians. They knew how to fight, and they knew the country well. But many on both sides still didn't understand that a revolution would grow from these brief battles.

One battle that the British lost was fought at the North Bridge near Concord. A Reverend William Emerson who lived nearby supported the Patriots. In 1847, his grandson wrote a hymn for the dedication of a battle monument there. He called the first shot at the bridge, "the shot heard round the world" because of the global implications it had, leading to American independence.

Summary:

By the bridge, farmers once stood with a flag. Under attack, they fired the shot heard round the world.

Now enemies and winners are long gone. So is the bridge.

Today we set a marker here, so their deed will be remembered when our sons are gone, like our fathers.

Spirit that drove these heroes, tell nature to treat gently the flag we raise to them, and to you.

Vocabulary:

bid = order

redeem = restore the honor of

rude = crude; rough

shaft = flag pole

sires = forefathers

unfurled = opened out

votive = expressing a pledge

Concord Hymn
by Ralph Waldo Emerson

By the rude bridge that arched the flood,
    Their flag to April's breeze unfurled,
Here once the embattled farmers stood
    And fired the shot heard round the world.

The foe long since in silence slept;
    Alike the conqueror silent sleeps;
And Time the ruined bridge has swept
    Down the dark stream which seaward
      creeps.

On this green bank, by this soft stream,
    We set today a votive stone;
That memory may their deed redeem,
    When, like our sires, our sons are gone.

Spirit, that made those heroes dare
    To die and leave their children free,
Bid time and Nature gently spare
    The shaft we raise to them and thee.

Source: Ralph Waldo Emerson, *Selected Prose and Poetry*. Reginald L. Cook, ed. New York: Holt, Rinehart and Winston, Inc., 1950, 1969, pp. 480-1.

The capture of Ft. Ticonderoga, showing Ethan Allen demanding that Captain De la Place surrenders.

May 1775—Ethan Allen at Ticonderoga

The colonial militia needed supplies. While the British were trapped in Boston, other Patriot troops advanced on Fort Ticonderoga in New York. It was an important location, and it held plenty of weapons, including cannons.

The raid was led by frontiersman Ethan Allen, leader of Vermont's Green Mountain Boys. Colonel Benedict Arnold was co-commander. However, Allen refused to let Arnold give orders to the troops. They took the fort.

Ethan Allen's speech to his men outside Fort Ticonderoga

Friends and fellow soldiers…your valor has been famed abroad…we must this morning either quit our pretensions to valor, or possess ourselves of this fortress in a few minutes. And inasmuch as it is a desperate attempt, which none but the bravest of men dare undertake, I do not urge it on any contrary to his will. You that will undertake voluntarily, poise your firelocks.

Source: Jeanne Munn Bracken, ed., *The Shot Heard 'Round the World: The Beginnings of the American Revolution.* Carlisle, MA: Discovery Enterprises, Ltd., 1995, p. 39.

Summary:

Your bravery is well-known everywhere. Now we must give up claims to courage, or take this fort quickly. It's reckless; only the bravest will try. I don't insist. Volunteers, ready your guns.

Vocabulary:

firelock = type of gun
inasmuch = since
pretensions = claim
poise = ready
quit = give up
undertake = try
valor = courage; bravery

June 1775—Bunker Hill

Young men rushed to Boston to join the action. John Trumbull was there.

Summary:

The army was a bunch of brave, eager, untrained lads; most officers were the same. Some old men had been soldiers, but not in the regular army.

Vocabulary:

assemblage = collection

irregular = soldier not in the regular military

John Trumbull, from his diary

The entire army, if it deserved the name, was but an assemblage of brave, enthusiastic, un-disciplined country lads; the officers, in general, quite as ignorant of military life as the troops, excepting a few elderly men, who had seen some irregular service....

Source: Jeanne Munn Bracken, ed., *The Shot Heard 'Round the World: The Beginnings of the American Revolution.* Carlisle, MA: Discovery Enterprises, Ltd., 1995, p. 43.

A panoramic view of Bunker Hill, published soon after the battle.

The first major battle was in Boston, on Breed's Hill. By mistake, it became known as the Battle of Bunker Hill (which was nearby). To save ammunition, Patriots were ordered to hold their fire until they could see "the whites of their eyes." When American's ammunition ran out, the British took the hill—but it cost them more than 1000 casualties.

The British held out in Boston for several more months. Meanwhile, the 43 cannon that Ethan Allen had captured at Fort Ticonderoga were hauled to Boston by ox team. When the Patriots installed those weapons on another hill near the city, the British gave up and left.

Yankee Doodle—A Joke that Backfired

Long before the official war began, British and Patriot soldiers made fun of each other. During the French and Indian War, a British surgeon wrote a song making fun of the colonists. It went with an old tune.

But the joke backfired. The Patriots liked the song so much they sang it themselves, all through the Revolutionary War. Some verses are below.

Yankee Doodle
by Richard Schuchburg,
British Army surgeon

Yankee Doodle went to town,
Riding on a pony;
Stuck a feather in his hat
And called it Macaroni.

(Chorus)
Yankee Doodle keep it up,
Yankee Doodle dandy;
Mind the music and the step,
And with the girls be handy.

Father and I went down to camp
Along with Captain Good'in,
And there we saw the men and boys
As thick as hasty puddin! *(Chorus)*

And there I saw a little keg,
Its head all made of leather,
They knocked on it with little sticks,
To call the folks together. *(Chorus)*

And there was Captain Washington
Upon a slapping stallion,
A-giving orders to his men;
I guess there was a million. *(Chorus)*

Commentary:
"Yankee" was an insult and "doodle" was a slang term meaning "fool." British uniforms had fancy trim—such as gold braid and ribbons—which they called "macaroni."

Vocabulary:
handy = skillful; expert
hasty pudding = a thick
   corn meal mush
keg = small barrel
slapping = first-class

Opinions and Concerns

The Second Continental Congress met in Philadelphia, beginning in May 1775. The members elected John Hancock president. They sent an appeal to King George, hoping to end the military conflict and work out a peaceful solution. But the king refused to even look at the paper. Instead, he declared the Americans to be in open rebellion. On June 15, Congress voted unanimously to appoint George Washington general and commander-in-chief of the new Continental Army.

The colonists always had varying ideas about what they should do about their problems with England.

Benjamin Franklin

Benjamin Franklin had loved England and thought it had an excellent government. He lived there for years as an agent for Pennsylvania. He made many efforts to smooth out the problems between England and the colonies. While returning home in 1775, he wrote a long letter to his son describing his conversations and efforts. The excerpt below expresses his feelings:

Commentary:

Mrs. Howe, an English woman, refers to the looming conflict as a civil war rather than a revolution. A civil war is fought between citizens of the same country. At this time, Franklin sometimes spoke of himself as English.

Vocabulary:

disposed = inclined
employ = hire; use
of service = of any use
practicable = possible; doable
reconciliation = settlement

Benjamin Franklin's letter to his son, 1775

[Mrs. Howe] said: "And what is to be done with this dispute between Great Britain and the colonies? I hope we are not to have a civil war." "They should kiss and be friends," said I; "what can they do better? Quarrelling can be of service to neither, but is ruin to both." "I have often said," replied she, "that I wished government would employ you to settle the dispute for 'em; I am sure nobody could do it so well. Do not you think the thing is practicable?" "Undoubtedly, madam, if the parties are disposed to reconciliation; for the two countries have really no clashing interests to differ about. 'Tis rather a matter …which two or three reasonable people might settle in half an hour."

Source: Carl Van Doren, ed., *Benjamin Franklin's Autobiographical Writings.* New York: Viking Press, 1945, p. 353.

Benjamin Franklin (*Leslie's Magazine*, special 100-year commemorative edition, 1887)

After Benjamin Franklin returned home from England, he became convinced that the situation wasn't going to be solved peacefully. He felt that the British Parliament was blind to the problems it created in the colonies. Franklin helped write the Declaration of Independence, and he also signed it.

In 1775, Franklin wrote a letter to a Tory friend in England expressing his change of position. (He never sent it.)

Franklin's letter to William Strahan

Mr. Strahan: You are a member of Parliament, and one of that majority which has doomed my country to destruction. You have begun to burn our towns and murder our people. Look upon your hands! They are stained with the blood of your relations! You and I were long friends. You are now my enemy, and I am

yours

B. Franklin

Source: Carl Van Doren, ed., *Benjamin Franklin's Autobiographical Writings*. New York: Viking Press, 1945, p. 406.

Summary:

You are one of the members of Parliament who has voted against my country. You have begun to burn and murder. Your hands are stained with our blood. We were friends, but now we are enemies.

Vocabulary:

majority = the greatest number

relations = relatives

Abigail Adams

Abigail Adams was the wife of John Adams, who would become the second president of the United States. She was the mother of John Quincy Adams, the sixth president. She had a lively mind and strong opinions. Abigail wrote to John in November, 1775, when he was in Philadelphia.

Summary:

I'm more sure than ever that man is dangerous. Power is always greedy. Like the grave, it wants more. Big fish swallow little ones.

If we are not British, what laws will we follow? How will we keep our liberty? I worry about the fate of our monarchy, democracy, or whatever else happens.

Vocabulary:

code = set of rules
grasping = greedy
monarchy = rule by a
   monarch (king, queen)
retain = keep
vested = given; settled

Abigail Adams' letter to John Adams

I am more and more convinced that man is a dangerous creature; and that power, whether vested in many or a few, is ever grasping, and, like the grave, cries "Give, Give." The great fish swallow up the small....

If we separate from Britain, what code of laws will be established? How shall we be governed so as to retain our liberties?... I feel anxious for the fate of our monarchy or democracy, or whatever is to take place.

Source: Abigail Adams' letter to John Adams in Philadelphia, November 27,1775. Found in *The Book of Abigail and John: Selected Letters of the Adams Family, 1762-1784,* eds.: L.H. Butterfield, Marc Friedlaender, and Mary-Jo Kline, Cambridge, MA: Harvard Press, 1975.

Thomas Paine

One thing that helped the members of Congress make up their minds to declare independence was a booklet that appeared in January of 1776. The author, Thomas Paine, was a recent immigrant from England, but he soon took up the Patriot's cause. He called this essay "Common Sense." It was read by hundreds of thousands of Americans—and it stirred many of them to action. Here is a brief excerpt.

From *Common Sense*
by Thomas Paine

The sun never shined on a cause of greater worth. 'Tis not the affair of a city, a county, a province, or a kingdom; but of a continent—of at least one eighth part of the habitable globe. 'Tis not the concern of a day, a year, or an age; posterity are virtually involved in the contest, and will be more or less affected even to the end of time, by the proceedings now....

I have heard it asserted by some, that as America has flourished under her former connection with Great Britain, the same connection is necessary towards her future happiness, and will always have the same effect. Nothing can be more fallacious than this kind of argument....

Everything that is right or reasonable pleads for separation. The blood of the slain...cries 'TIS TIME TO PART.

Source: Thomas Paine, *Rights of Man, Common Sense, and Other Political Writings.* Mark Philp, ed., Oxford: Oxford University Press, 1995.

Summary:

There was never a more worthwhile cause. This isn't just about the present. Our descendants are as good as involved. They will be affected forever by what happens now.

I have heard some say that America did well under Great Britain, and should stay connected for our future happiness. This is a terrible argument.

The blood of the dead cries out for us to part.

Vocabulary:

affair = business
asserted = insisted
fallacious = misleading
flourished = done well
habitable = livable
posterity = descendants
proceedings = actions; events
province = similar to a state
virtually = practically; almost

July 1776—Making a Statement

In May, 1776, King Louis XIV of France promised military supplies for the American troops. Spain also agreed to help. But now the British were putting on pressure. Their war fleet arrived in New York Harbor, with 30 battleships and 300 supply ships. They carried 30,000 soldiers, 10,000 sailors, and 1,200 cannon. The British troops were commanded by General William Howe and his brother, Admiral Lord Richard Howe. Meanwhile, in Charleston, South Carolina, American forces fought off a British naval attack.

In June, a resolution in the Continental Congress called for a formal declaration of independence from Britain. Congress appointed John Adams, Thomas Jefferson, Benjamin Franklin, and two others to prepare the document. The actual writing was mostly left to Jefferson, the committee chairman.

Thomas Jefferson, after a print by Desnoyers

John Adams, from a portrait by Gilbert Stuart

Thomas Jefferson

Thomas Jefferson was a member of the Second Continental Congress. He would later be governor of Virginia, U.S. minister to France, secretary of state under George Washington, vice-president under John Adams, and president of the United States. But he was proudest of his work on the Declaration. In June of 1776, Jefferson sent a copy of his work to Franklin, with a note asking for his input. Franklin, other committee members, and the Congress all worked on the document too.

John Adams

John Adams was committed to American independence ten years before the Revolutionary War. However, he believed so strongly in a fair justice system for all, that he defended the British soldiers accused of the Boston Massacre. Adams would be the first vice-president and then the second president of the United States

In Philadelphia, the Continental Congress was trying to answer some of the same questions that bothered Abigail Adams. On July 3, 1776, John wrote to her. He was two days off on his prediction for Independence Day.

John Adams' letter to Abigail Adams

Yesterday the greatest question was decided which ever was debated in America, and a greater, perhaps, never was nor will be decided among men. A resolution was passed without one dissenting colony, "that the United Colonies are, and of right ought to be, free and independent States...." You will see in a few days a Declaration setting forth the causes which have impelled us to this mighty revolution, and the reasons which will justify it in the sight of God and man....

The second day of July, 1776, will be the most memorable...in the history of America. I ...believe that it will be celebrated by succeeding generations as the great anniversary festival. It ought to be commemorated...by solemn acts of devotion to God Almighty [and] with pomp and parade, with shows, games, sports, guns, bells, bonfires and illuminations, from one end of this continent to the other, from this time forward, forevermore.

Source: Abigail Adams and John Adams, *The Book of Abigail and John: Selected Letters of the Adams Family, 1762-1784.* L.H. Butterfield, Marc Friedlaender, and Mary-Jo Kline, eds., Cambridge MA: Harvard Press, 1975, pp. 139-40.

Summary:

Yesterday we made the most important decision for America. A resolution for independence passed without one vote against it. You'll soon see a Declaration explaining the reasons. July 2, 1776 will be the most memorable day in American history. I think it will be celebrated by following generations, with devotion, parades, shows, games, noise, bonfires, and fireworks.

Vocabulary:
dissenting = disagreeing
commemorated = honored
illuminations = lights; fireworks
impelled = driven
pomp = dignified display
resolution = statement
setting forth = laying out
solemn = serious
succeeding = following

In CONGRESS, July 4, 1776.

A DECLARATION

By the REPRESENTATIVES OF THE

UNITED STATES OF AMERICA,

In GENERAL CONGRESS ASSEMBLED.

WHEN in the Courfe of human Events, it becomes neceffary for one People to diffolve the Political Bands which have connected them with another, and to affume among the Powers of the Earth, the feparate and equal Station to which the Laws of Nature, and of Nature's God entitle them, a decent Refpect to the Opinions of Mankind requires that they fhould declare the caufes which impel them to the Separation.

We hold thefe Truths to be felf-evident, that all Men are created equal, that they are endowed by their Creator with certain unalienable Rights, that among thefe are Life, Liberty, and the Purfuit of Happinefs—That to fecure thefe Rights, Governments are inftituted among Men, deriving their juft Powers from the Confent of the Governed, that whenever any Form of Government becomes deftructive of thefe Ends, it is the Right of the People to alter or to abolifh it, and to inftitute new Government, laying its Foundation on fuch Principles, and organizing its Powers in fuch Form, as to them fhall feem moft likely to effect their Safety and Happinefs. Prudence, indeed, will dictate that Governments long eftablifhed fhould not be changed for light and tranfient Caufes; and accordingly all Experience hath fhewn, that Mankind are more difpofed to fuffer, while Evils are fufferable, than to right themfelves by abolifhing the Forms to which they are accuftomed. But when a long Train of Abufes and Ufurpations, purfuing invariably the fame Object, evinces a Defign to reduce them under abfolute Defpotifm, it is their Right, it is their Duty, to throw off fuch Government, and to provide new Guards for their future Security. Such has been the patient Sufferance of thefe Colonies; and fuch is now the Neceffity which conftrains them to alter their former Syftems of Government. The Hiftory of the prefent King of Great-Britain is a Hiftory of repeated Injuries and Ufurpations, all having in direct Object the Eftablifhment of an abfolute Tyranny over thefe States. To prove this, let Facts be fubmitted to a candid World.

He has refufed his Affent to Laws, the moft wholefome and neceffary for the public Good.

He has forbidden his Governors to pafs Laws of immediate and preffing Importance, unlefs fufpended in their Operation till his Affent fhould be obtained; and when fo fufpended, he has utterly neglected to attend to them.

He has refufed to pafs other Laws for the Accommodation of large Diftricts of People, unlefs thofe People would relinquifh the Right of Reprefentation in the Legiflature, a Right ineftimable to them, and formidable to Tyrants only.

He has called together Legiflative Bodies at Places unufual, uncomfortable, and diftant from the Depofitory of their public Records, for the fole Purpofe of fatiguing them into Compliance with his Meafures.

He has diffolved Reprefentative Houfes repeatedly, for oppofing with manly Firmnefs his Invafions on the Rights of the People.

He has refufed for a long Time, after fuch Diffolutions, to caufe others to be elected; whereby the Legiflative Powers, incapable of Annihilation, have returned to the People at large for their exercife; the State remaining in the mean time expofed to all the Dangers of Invafion from without, and Convulfions within.

He has endeavoured to prevent the Population of thefe States; for that Purpofe obftructing the Laws for Naturalization of Foreigners; refufing to pafs others to encourage their Migrations hither, and raifing the Conditions of new Appropriations of Lands.

He has obftructed the Adminiftration of Juftice, by refufing his Affent to Laws for eftablifhing Judiciary Powers.

He has made Judges dependent on his Will alone, for the Tenure of their Offices, and the Amount and Payment of their Salaries.

He has erected a Multitude of new Offices, and fent hither Swarms of Officers to harrafs our People, and eat out their Subftance.

He has kept among us, in Times of Peace, Standing Armies, without the confent of our Legiflatures.

He has affected to render the Military independent of and fuperior to the Civil Power.

He has combined with others to fubject us to a Jurifdiction foreign to our Conftitution, and unacknowledged by our Laws; giving his Affent to their Acts of pretended Legiflation:

For quartering large Bodies of Armed Troops among us:

For protecting them, by a mock Trial, from Punifhment for any Murders which they fhould commit on the Inhabitants of thefe States:

For cutting off our Trade with all Parts of the World:

For impofing Taxes on us without our Confent:

For depriving us, in many Cafes, of the Benefits of Trial by Jury:

For transporting us beyond Seas to be tried for pretended Offences:

For abolifhing the free Syftem of Englifh Laws in a neighbouring Province, eftablifhing therein an arbitrary Government, and enlarging its Boundaries, fo as to render it at once an Example and fit Inftrument for introducing the fame abfolute Rule into thefe Colonies:

For taking away our Charters, abolifhing our moft valuable Laws, and altering fundamentally the Forms of our Governments:

For fufpending our own Legiflatures, and declaring themfelves invefted with Power to legiflate for us in all Cafes whatfoever.

He has abdicated Government here, by declaring us out of his Protection and waging War againft us.

He has plundered our Seas, ravaged our Coafts, burnt our Towns, and deftroyed the Lives of our People.

He is, at this Time, tranfporting large Armies of foreign Mercenaries to compleat the Works of Death, Defolation, and Tyranny, already begun with circumftances of Cruelty and Perfidy, fcarcely paralleled in the moft barbarous Ages, and totally unworthy the Head of a civilized Nation.

He has conftrained our fellow Citizens taken Captive on the high Seas to bear Arms againft their Country, to become the Executioners of their Friends and Brethren, or to fall themfelves by their Hands.

He has excited domeftic Infurrections amongft us, and has endeavoured to bring on the Inhabitants of our Frontiers, the mercilefs Indian Savages, whofe known Rule of Warfare, is an undiftinguifhed Deftruction, of all Ages, Sexes and Conditions.

In every ftage of thefe Oppreffions we have Petitioned for Redrefs in the moft humble Terms: Our repeated Petitions have been anfwered only by repeated Injury. A Prince, whofe Character is thus marked by every act which may define a Tyrant, is unfit to be the Ruler of a free People.

Nor have we been wanting in Attentions to our Britifh Brethren. We have warned them from Time to Time of Attempts by their Legiflature to extend an unwarrantable Jurifdiction over us. We have reminded them of the Circumftances of our Emigration and Settlement here. We have appealed to their native Juftice and Magnanimity, and we have conjured them by the Ties of our common Kindred to difavow thefe Ufurpations, which, would inevitably interrupt our Connections and Correfpondence. They too have been deaf to the Voice of Juftice and of Confanguinity. We muft, therefore, acquiefce in the Neceffity, which denounces our Separation, and hold them, as we hold the reft of Mankind, Enemies in War, in Peace, Friends.

We, therefore, the Reprefentatives of the UNITED STATES OF AMERICA, in GENERAL CONGRESS, Affembled, appealing to the Supreme Judge of the World for the Rectitude of our Intentions, do, in the Name, and by Authority of the good People of thefe Colonies, folemnly Publifh and Declare, That thefe United Colonies are, and of Right ought to be, FREE AND INDEPENDENT STATES; that they are abfolved from all Allegiance to the Britifh Crown, and that all political Connection between them and the State of Great-Britain, is and ought to be totally diffolved; and that as FREE AND INDEPENDENT STATES, they have full Power to levy War, conclude Peace, contract Alliances, eftablifh Commerce, and to do all other Acts and Things which INDEPENDENT STATES may of right do. And for the fupport of this Declaration, with a firm Reliance on the Protection of divine Providence, we mutually pledge to each other our Lives, our Fortunes, and our facred Honor.

Signed by ORDER and in BEHALF of the CONGRESS,

JOHN HANCOCK, President.

Declaration of Independence, typeset by John Dunlap. (Library of Congress)

On July 4, 1776, Congress voted to accept the Declaration. The typeset copy above appeared on July 5. The version we usually see, with fancy handwritten letters, wasn't available for signing until August 2.

What Did the Declaration Mean?

Originally, writing a Declaration of Independence was just a practical matter. The Continental Congress needed to make a statement of their intentions. For the next 20 years or so, the document wasn't given much attention. But during the 1790s, it was often read aloud at Fourth of July celebrations. Thomas Jefferson was pleased about that. Near the end of his life, in 1825, Jefferson wrote a letter discussing the document.

Thomas Jefferson's letter to Henry Lee

This was the object of the Declaration of Independence. Not to find out new principles, or new arguments, never before thought of, not merely to say things which had never been said before; but to place before mankind the common sense of the subject, in terms so plain and firm as to command their assent, and to justify ourselves in the independent stand we are compelled to take. Neither aiming at originality of principle or sentiment, nor yet copied from any particular and previous writing, it was intended to be an expression of the American mind, and to give to that expression the proper tone and spirit called for by the occasion.

Source: Thomas Jefferson, *Writings*. Merrill D. Peterson, ed., New York: Library of America, 1984, p. 1501.

Summary:

This was the purpose of the Declaration of Independence. Not to reveal new truths or arguments that hadn't been thought of before. It wasn't to say things that hadn't been said before. It was to show common sense about the situation. We wanted to speak plainly and firmly, to get others to agree and to justify our actions. We didn't try for original truths or feelings. But it wasn't copied from anything else. It was intended to express the American mind, with the right style and spirit for the occasion.

Vocabulary:
assent = agreement
discover = reveal
principles = basic truths; laws
sentiment = feeling; attitude
tone = effect

A Change of Flags

Even when the colonies declared their independence, their first flag looked very British. The Continental Colors had the familiar 13 red and white stripes representing the 13 colonies. But it had the British Union Jack where we now have stars. Since many English flags had red and white stripes, this wasn't much of a break with the past. It seemed like a flag that might be flown by British citizens who simply wanted some changes made.

In June of 1777, the Continental Congress decided that the flag of the United States would have the 13 stripes, and also 13 white stars on a blue field. Stars were unusual on flags in those days, and no one knows why Congress chose them. This flag seemed more like one that might be flown by an independent nation. Over the next two centuries, it would go through more design changes—but the stars and strips were there to stay.

War

In July of 1776, the British sailed two ships up the Hudson River, blasting their guns all the way. Then the British said they would be merciful if the Americans would like to give up now. Washington politely refused.

Supply Problems

The American army always had serious problems with supplies. There was never enough food, clothing, tents, arms, or ammunition. And there was never enough money to buy what was needed. Part of the problem was that the new government wasn't really used to working together. Members of the Continental Congress represented 13 states—which had very recently been 13 separate colonies.

Resolution of the Continental Congress, November, 1775

Resolved, That a ration consist of the following kind and quantity of provisions…

1 lb. of beef, or 3/4 lb. pork, or 1 lb. salt fish, per day.

1 lb. of bread or flour per day.

3 pints of pease, or beans per week, or vegitables equivalent, at one dollar per bushel for pease or beans.

1 pint of milk per man per day, or at the rate of 1/72 of a dollar.

1 half pint of Rice, or 1 pint of indian meal per man per week.

1 quart of spruce beer or cyder per man per day, or nine gallons of Molasses per company of 100 men per week.

3 lb. candles to 100 Men per week for guards.

24 lb. of soft or 8 lb. of hard soap for 100 men per week.

Source: Frank E. Grizzard, Jr., "Supply Problems Plagued the Continental Army from the Beginning." In *The Papers of George Washington,* http://www.virginia.edu/gwpapers/html

Commentary:
The Continental Congress arrived at this list of basic rations for each soldier. They also ordered such things as blankets, fabric for uniforms, weapons, and medical supplies.

Vocabulary:
cyder = cider
equivalent = in an equal amount
indian meal = ground corn
pease = peas
vegitables = vegetables

1776—Defeats and Retreats

General Howe led 15,000 soldiers against Washington's army at Long Island, New York. Outnumbered two-to-one, the Americans were badly defeated. They retreated, but were still in danger of being captured or forced to surrender completely. The Revolutionary War could have ended right then and there. But one foggy night, the Americans slipped away from the British threat. They crossed the East River in small boats and escaped to Manhattan.

"The Retreat from Brooklyn Heights" to New York, led by Washington. British officers later regarded this retreat as one of the most remarkable feats in military history, because of the success of such a massive maneuver under such desperate conditions in so short a time.

After the loss at Long Island, General Washington changed his battle plans. To avoid a direct fight with the huge British force, he made a series of retreats. In September, the Americans turned back a British attack in upper Manhattan.

However, in October the American navy suffered a big defeat on Lake Champlain. The inexperienced Patriots were no match for the British fleet. The Americans lost 83 gunships in just a few days.

In the next few battles, Washington's troops again suffered heavy losses. British General Howe captured over 100 cannon, and thousands of muskets and cartridges.

September, 1776—Washington's Worries

George Washington was worried about his troops—how to keep them, and how to enlist more and better men. He wrote to the President of the Continental Congress, John Hancock.

Washington's letter to Congress, September 24, 1776

Sir: From the hours allotted to Sleep, I will borrow a few Moments to convey my thoughts on sundry important matters to Congress.... unless some speedy, and effectual measures are adopted by Congress, our cause will be lost. It is in vain to expect, that any (or more than a trifling) part of this Army will again engage in the Service on the encouragement offered by Congress.... the Congress will deceive themselves therefore if they expect it. A Soldier... hears you with patience, and acknowledges the truth of your observations, but adds, that it is of no more Importance to him than others. The Officer makes you the same reply, with this further remark, that his pay will not support him, and he cannot ruin himself and Family.... It becomes evidently clear then, that as this Contest is not likely to be the Work of a day...you must have good Officers, there are, in my Judgment, no other possible means to obtain them but by establishing your Army upon a permanent footing; and giving your Officers good pay....

Source: Text prepared by George Welling for *The American Revolution—an .HTML project.* Found at http://www.let.rug.nl/~usa/P/gw1/writings/brf/recruit.htm

Summary:

Instead of sleeping, I'll tell you about some important matters. Unless Congress acts quickly and well, our cause is lost. It's foolish to think that many soldiers will serve for what they get. A soldier listens patiently, but tells you that this cause is not the most important thing to him. The officer says the same, and adds that he cannot ruin his family. Since this war will be long, you must have good officers. The only way is to create a permanent army and pay your Officers well.

Vocabulary:

acknowledges = admits
allotted = set aside for
convey = communicate
effectual = effective; workable
establishing = setting up; creating
evidently = obviously
sundry = various
systematically = step-by-step
vain, in vain = useless

Christmas, 1776—Counterattack

After the American losses, Washington retreated toward the Delaware River. The British General Cornwallis pursued him. Washington took his troops across the river into Pennsylvania. The British advanced. To avoid capture, the Continental Congress left Philadelphia and went to Baltimore, Maryland.

Then Washington made a surprise move. Using every small boat they could find, Washington took 2400 men back across the river. They surprised 1500 British and German troops at Trenton, New Jersey. The Americans took 1000 prisoners and only lost 6 men.

Detail of "Washington Crossing the Delaware." American artist Emmanuel Leutze posed friends for his famous 1851 painting.

January 1777—Another Victory, But a Long Winter

Patriot troops defeated the British at Princeton, New Jersey. Washington set up headquarters at Morristown, New Jersey. However, that winter was harsh. Many soldiers whose enlistments expired didn't sign up again. Others deserted. In the spring, the army finally began to grow again as new recruits arrived.

The Continental Congress returned to Philadelphia. However, in September, 1777, both American and British troops suffered heavy losses in a battle at Brandywine Creek. Washington's troops were forced back toward Philadelphia. Once again, Congress had to move—this time to Lancaster, Pennsylvania.

Desperate Soldiers

Washington's troops were still poorly equipped. They asked for donations from citizens—and some of what they took wasn't actually offered. The Quakers were pacifists, so the troops usually didn't turn to them for help. (Pacifists oppose violence as a way of settling disputes.) As the following two accounts show, a Philadelphia Quaker saw what others went through, and a teenage girl found the retreating American troops rather frightening.

Elizabeth Drinker – a Quaker woman's account

Many [citizens] have had their Horses taken from them this afternoon; some going one way, and some another.... All ye Bells in ye city are Certainly taken away, and there is talk of Pump handles and Fire-Buckets being taken also—but that may be only conjecture.

Source: Sally Smith Booth, *The Women of '76*. New York: Hastings House Publishers, 1973, p. 145.

Summary:
Many horses were taken, one way or another. All the bells are gone, and they say pump handles and fire buckets, too—but that may be just a guess.

Vocabulary:
conjecture = guesswork
ye = the

Sally Wister– a teenager's description

About seven o'clock we heard a great noise. To the door we all went. A large number of waggons, with about three hundred of the Philadelphia Militia. They begged for drink, and several push'd into the house. One of those that entered was a little tipsy, and had a mind to be saucy.

I then thought it time for me to retreat...but after a while, seeing the officers appear gentlemanly, and the soldiers civil, I call'd reason to my aid. My fears were in some measure dispell'd, tho my teeth rattled and my hand shook like an aspen leaf.

Source: Sally Smith Booth, *The Women of '76*. New York: Hastings House Publishers, 1973, pp. 145-6.

Summary:
There were lots of wagons and soldiers. They wanted a drink, and some pushed in. One was a little drunk and bold.
I started to leave, but the officers were polite. The soldiers were all right. I thought again and felt better, but I still shook.

Vocabulary:
aspen = a tree with leaves that quiver in the wind
call'd = called
civil = not rude
dispell'd = dispelled
saucy = forward, rude
waggons = wagons

October, 1777—Sending the Enemy Home

The Patriots first real victory was the Battle of Saratoga. Generals Horatio Gates and Benedict Arnold defeated the British General Burgoyne. Over 5000 captured British men were put onto ships and sent back to England.

Burgoyne surrenders to Gates, Saratoga, October17, 1777

Winter 1777-1778—Death at Valley Forge

Washington camped at Valley Forge, near Philadelphia. Poorly fed, housed, and clothed, the soldiers were cold and hungry. That winter, 2500 men died.

Summary:

There's a soldier with feet showing through his shoes, torn stockings, not enough pants left to cover him, shirt in strings, hair a mess, face thin. He cries, "I am sick, lame, sore, and itching. I will die soon. And all I'll get is someone mentioning it.

Vocabulary:

dishevell'd = dishevelled; disordered

meagre = meager; lean

tatter'd = tattered; ragged

Diary of a Surgeon at Valley Forge
by Albigence Waldo

There comes a Soldier, his bare feet are seen thro' his worn out Shoes, his legs nearly naked from the tatter'd remains of an only pair of stockings, his Breeches not sufficient to cover his nakedness, his Shirt hanging in Strings, his hair dishevell'd, his face meagre.... He comes, and crys...I am Sick, my feet lame, my legs are sore, my body cover'd with this tormenting Itch.... I fail fast I shall soon be no more! and all the reward I shall get will be—"Poor Will is dead."

Source: Vakgroep Alfa-Informatica, Rijksuniversiteit Groningen, Department of Humanities Computing http://grid.let.rug.nl/~usa/D/1776-1800/war/waldo.htm

Nathan Hale was caught spying for the Patriots. When he was hanged, his last words were "I only regret that I have but one life to lose for my country." There was never a portrait painted of Hale, so no one can be sure what he really looked like.

Spies

From the very beginning of the problems between American colonists and the British, both sides had spies. Even before the battles at Lexington and Concord, Loyalists were watching to see where the Patriots had hidden their weapons. Patriots were watching to see when the British would try to find those weapons—and whether they were getting close.

After the war began, General Washington needed information on British troop strength and plans. In 1776, a former schoolteacher named Nathan Hale volunteered. Traveling behind British lines, he identified himself as a schoolteacher rather than a soldier.

Hale got the information Washington needed, but he was caught on his way back to the Patriot troops. He may have been betrayed by a Loyalist relative. The British General Howe didn't put Nathan Hale on trial—he simply hanged him the next morning.

Other spies were more successful. Women also spied for Patriots and for Loyalists. They helped trapped soldiers escape, got important information, and carried messages.

Deborah Champion Rides

Deborah Champion was the daughter of an American Colonel. In 1776, when she was 22, Deborah was asked to carry important messages to General Washington. Everyone hoped that a woman traveling with a servant would be ignored by British guards.

Summary:

I knew I couldn't avoid the British without losing too much time. I summoned my courage and hid my papers in the saddlebag. They were under food that Mother had packed. I planned to ride all night. Very early in the morning, a sentry stopped me. I pulled my bonnet down over my face. My servant was frightened, but if I was held he would go on. A soldier took me to headquarters, but I said it was too early to wake up the captain. I said I had been sent in a hurry to see a friend in need. That was true in a way. He let me go because he thought I was just an old woman.

Vocabulary:

ambiguous = more than
  one possible meaning
detained = held
muster = call up; summon
plucked up = summoned
secreting = hiding

Deborah Champion's account

I heard that it would be almost impossible to avoid the British unless by going so far out of the way that too much time would be lost, so I plucked up what courage I could and secreting my papers in a small pocket in the saddlebags, under all the eatables mother had filled them with, I rode on, determined to ride all night. It was late at night, or rather very early in the morning, that I heard the call of the sentry and knew that now, if at all, the danger point was reached, but pulling my [bonnet] still farther over my face, I went on with what boldness I could muster. Suddenly I was ordered to halt; as I couldn't help myself, I did so. I could almost hear [my servant's] teeth rattle in his mouth, but I knew he would obey my instructions and if I was detained would try to find the way alone. A soldier in a red coat proceeded to take me to headquarters, but I told him it was early to wake the captain, and to please to let me pass for I had been sent in urgent haste to see a friend in need, which was true if ambiguous. To my joy, he let me go, saying, "Well, you are only an old woman anyway," evidently as glad to get rid of me as I of him.

Source: Sally Smith Booth, *The Women of '76*. New York: Hastings House Publishers, 1973, pp. 55-7.

Benedict Arnold's Code

As an American general, Benedict Arnold helped to win some important battles. However, he felt that he never got enough credit for his accomplishments. Bitter and in need of money, he began passing information to the British in 1779. After his spying was discovered in 1780, he led British troops in two raids. He later moved to London.

Spies on both sides used secret codes. Benedict Arnold used a cipher—letters, numbers, or symbols used in place of the real words. He found the words he wanted to use in a published book. In his message, he wrote down the page number, the line number, and the number of the word, counting from the left. For example, the second word in the letter of July 12, 1780, is "293.9.7" which stands for "wrote."

For more about the codes that Arnold and other spies used in the Revolutionary War, see the web site in the source below.

I 293.9.7 to C_t. B. 103.8.2. the 7th 152.9.17. that, a F__ 112.9.17. and 22.8.29 were 105.9.50 to / 4 9.71 in 62.8.20 with, 163.8.19 A 22.8.19 at with 230.8.13. 263.8.17 I gave Mr. S---y a 164.8.16 / 147.8.261 to be 209.9.216 in C----a and have from 163.8.17 to .163.8.17 .58.8.27 to him. / Such 147.8.21 as I 164.9.5

Above are the first few sentences of a letter written by Benedict Arnold to John André on July 12, 1780. The message makes use of a secret code. This is a typeset version. The actual handwritten letter can be seen on the web site. On the right is the first paragraph of the decoded message.

Source: http://www.si.umich.edu/spies/ Click on "Gallery of Letters," Benedict Arnold to John Andre, July 12, 1780. From The Clinton Collection: Spy Letters of the American Revolution.

I wrote to Captn B[eckwith]-on the 7th of June, that a F[rench]--- fleet and army / were expected to act in conjunction with the A[merican]---army. At the same time / I gave Mr. S[tansbury]-a manifesto intended to be published in C[anad]---a, and have / from time to time communicated to him such intelligence as I thought / interesting, which he assures me he has transmitted to you. I have / received no answer from my Letter, or any verbal Message – I expect soon / to command W[est] P[oin]t and most seriously wish an interview with some / intelligent officer in whom a mutual confidence could be placed. The / necessity is evident to arrange and to cooperate– An officer might / be taken Prisoner near that Post and permitted to return on parole, / or some officer on Parole sent out to effect an exchange.

A World War

The war between the American colonies and the British also involved people from other countries. At the start of the war, the British hired German mercenaries to increase their armies. (A mercenary is a soldier hired to fight for a foreign army.) The "Hessians" contributed greatly to the British effort.

In 1777, a young French nobleman arrived in Philadelphia and volunteered to fight for the Americans without pay. The Marquis de Lafayette became one of Washington's most trusted aides. He was only 19 at the time. A Prussian general named Baron von Steuben came to Valley Forge and gave Washington's troops training they badly needed. (Prussia was a kingdom with its capital at Berlin.)

The French gave the Americans military aid, and in 1778, France officially recognized the United States. Then British ships fired on French ships, and the two nations declared war on each other. In 1779, Spain declared war on England. The Dutch continued to trade with France and America, and the British declared war on them too. So the British were at war on many different fronts.

Native Americans also got involved. They generally sided with the British, who had forbidden colonists to settle west of the Appalachian mountains. In 1778, the Iroquois terrorized frontier settlements. At different times and places, both Loyalists and Indians massacred colonists and burned towns.

Several times during the war, the British suggested terms for peace. But they always insisted that America give up independence—and that was always rejected. In September of 1779, John Adams was appointed by Congress to negotiate a peace with England on better terms. Meanwhile, Benjamin Franklin was in France, representing the United States.

June 1778—The Battle of Monmouth

At Monmouth, New Jersey, American troops faced the British under General Clinton. George Washington decided that this was the time to strike a strong blow. He ordered General Charles Lee to attack the British from the rear. However, during the fighting, Lee ordered a retreat. Even so, Washington's troops fought the British to a draw. But Lee's action—or lack of it—gave the British time to withdraw. Washington was furious with Lee, who was later court-martialed for disobeying orders.

The Battle of Monmouth was fought in scorching hot weather. Mary Ludwig Hayes, the wife of an American soldier, became a legend that day.

During the Battle of Monmouth Court House, Molly Pitcher took over at the cannon which had been manned by her fallen husband.

Molly Pitcher

Mary Ludwig Hayes became known as "Molly Pitcher," because she carried pitcher after pitcher of cool water to the artillerymen and the wounded. A soldier who described her said that she also helped load one of the cannons.

A Narrative about Molly Pitcher

While in the act of reaching a cartridge and having one of her feet as far before the other as she could step, a cannon shot from the enemy passed directly between her legs without doing any other damage than carrying away all the lower part of her petticoat. Looking at it with apparent unconcern, she observed that it was lucky it did not pass a little higher, for in that case it might have carried away something else, and continued her occupation.

Source: Richard Wheeler, *Voices of 1776*. New York: Thomas Y. Crowell Company, 1972. Reprinted from *A Narrative of Some of the Adventures, Dangers and Sufferings of a Revolutionary Soldier* by Joseph Plumb Martin, Hallowell, Maine; 1830.

Summary:

Reaching for a cartridge, she stood with one foot far in front of the other. Suddenly, an enemy cannonball passed right between her legs. It only tore off the bottom of her petticoat. Unconcerned, she just went on with her work.

Vocabulary:

cartridge = a casing containing the explosive for ammunition

petticoat = slip; underskirt

The Bon Homme Richard *battling with the British ship* HMS Serapis. (From encarta.msn.com/find)

September 1779—John Paul Jones Fights On

John Paul Jones named his ship the *Bon Homme Richard,* after Benjamin Franklin (and his *Poor Richard's Almanac*). Near England, Jones led several other ships in raids on English shipping. The British ship, *HMS Serapis,* blasted the *Bon Homme Richard,* destroying many guns and gunners. But when the British captain asked whether Jones surrendered, the American replied "I have not yet begun to fight!" Even though their ship was sinking, Jones and his crew fought on until the British captain surrendered. The *Bon Homme Richard* sank the next day, but Jones and his crew moved to the *Serapis.*

Mutinies among the Troops

Even though George Washington and others made efforts to supply the army properly, something was always lacking. Food was often scarce, and sometimes the men weren't paid for months. Every winter, many soldiers deserted. However, George Washington was good at keeping most of his army together.

Several times there were mutinies. (A mutiny is a rebellion against those in command.) Some mutinies were settled by negotiation, and others were put down only by bringing in loyal Patriot forces. In New Jersey, two protest leaders were hanged. After a mutiny was over, many of those who participated often left the army.

May 1780—Loss at Charleston

Americans had their worst defeat of the entire war when the British captured Charleston, South Carolina. The entire southern American army of 5400 men was taken prisoner. The British also captured four ships and a military arsenal. (An arsenal is a place where weapons and ammunition are stored.)

During most of the war, Charleston and other cities had problems with outlaw looters. Sometimes they came back again and again, taking whatever they wanted from the Patriots' houses, businesses, and farms.

Eliza Wilkinson's letter to a friend about the looting at her house

I [spoke] to the inhumane monster who had my clothes. [I said] we could not replace what they'd taken from us...but I got nothing but a curse for my pains... Casting his eyes toward my shoes: "I want them buckles."... A brother villain, whose enormous mouth extended from ear to ear, bawled out: "Shares there, I say; Shares." So they divided my buckles between them.... They took my sister's ear-rings from her ears; hers, Miss Samuell's buckles; they demanded her ring from her finger...

We have been...again plundered, worse than ever plundered! Our very doors and window shutters were taken from the house, and carried aboard the vessels which lay in the river opposite our habitation....

Source: Sally Smith Booth, *The Women of '76*. New York: Hastings House Publishers, 1973, pp. 258-9.

Summary:

I told the monster who had my clothes that we couldn't replace what they took. His reply was a curse. He saw my shoe buckles and wanted them. His friends demanded they share, so they divided them. They took earrings, buckles, a ring from her finger....

Now we've been robbed again, worse than ever. Even our doors and windows were taken.

Vocabulary:
casting = turning
habitation = residence
inhumane = without pity
plundered = robbed by force
vessels = boats
villain = wicked or evil person

1780-1781—Guerilla War in the South

Over the next year, the Americans and British traded success and defeats. General Cornwallis led the British troops in the south.

In October of 1780, General Nathanael Greene was put in command of the southern American army. He changed their fighting style. Greene led the enemy on a wild chase through the rough hills of the Carolinas and Virginia. The British, led by Cornwallis, were worn down by Greene's guerilla warfare. (In guerilla warfare, small bands of troops make surprise raids on the enemy, then slip away.)

Cornwallis and 10,000 men finally withdrew to Yorktown, Virginia, to rest. In New York, George Washington received a letter saying that the French fleet was going to the Chesapeake Bay (in Maryland and Virginia). Washington organized his troops and headed for Virginia. He set up a siege at Yorktown. French ships bombarded the British from the water. Patriot troops tightened the circle.

October, 1781—Silent Guns at Yorktown

The Americans moved closer and closer to Yorktown, digging new trenches every night. All the while, the British were firing at them. Sarah Osborne was there with her soldier husband.

Summary:

We kept digging. Enemy fire was heavy until morning. Then it stopped. The enemy drums beat harder than usual.

Suddenly the officers cheered. Sarah asked "What is the matter?"

One replied, "Aren't you soldier enough to know?"

When she said no, they told her, "The British have surrendered."

Vocabulary:

excessively = more than normal

Sarah Osborne's account of the war

While digging...the enemy fired very heavy till about nine o'clock the next morning, then stopped, and the drums from the enemy beat excessively....

The drums continued beating, and all at once the officers hurrahed and swung their hats, and [I] asked them, "What is the matter now?"

One of them replied, "Are you not soldier enough to know what it means?"

[I] replied, "No."

They then replied, "The British have surrendered."

Source: John C. Dann, ed., *The Revolution Remembered: Eyewitness Accounts of the War For Independence.* Chicago: The University of Chicago Press, 1980, p. 249.

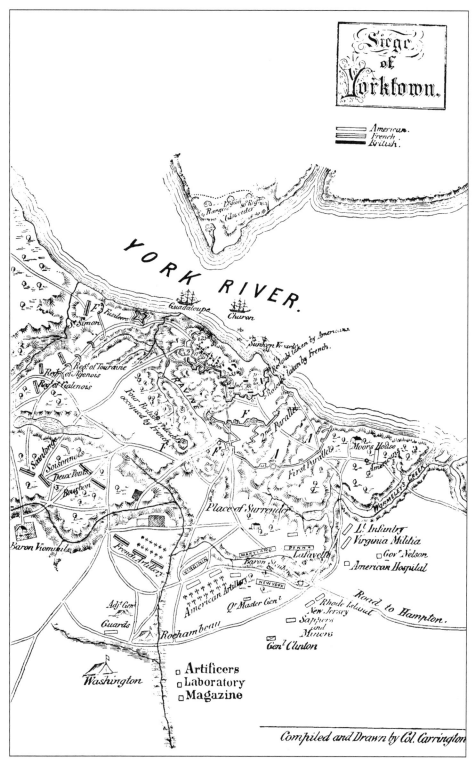

Map of the siege of Yorktown

1782—End in Sight

Despite the fact that the British and the Americans had had their final battle in South Carolina, the fighting wasn't completely over. In some places, Patriot forces massacred Native Americans, taking revenge for their earlier slaughter of settlers. In other places, Indians still conducted raids.

The most famous Indian atrocity of the Revolution was the murder of Jane McCrea by Indians fighting with Burgoyne in 1777.

Americans retaliated against the Indians by burning their villages.

The final military action of the war actually had taken place between the French and British fleets off Cape Henry on September 5, 1781. The Americans were not even part of the conflict. Here the French secured the control of the sea off Yorktown, forcing the British to head north. The American and French armies continued to pound the British...[making Cornwallis's surrender inevitable.]

The loss at Yorktown convinced the British that they couldn't win the war. Loyalists began moving to England; weary soldiers yearned for home.

Samuell Searls' letter to his mother, May 12th 1782

We hear...more than two thirds of [the new Parliament] voted for america which gives us a great reason to think that Peace will be settled by next fall—and we dont expect to [fight] this year—the times is exceeding hard hear among us we draw no wages and are not like to draw any this summer—but I hope the war will be over next fall. Pray Dear mothr be so kind as to give my love to all...at home and tell them, I determining to come home next fall if I live and see them once more and enjoy my self as well as those people that are their—for because we are...venturing our lives to defend them they have forgot us—but their is a day a coming that they will be obliged to minde us and pay us our just due.... Dear mother I think it very hard that the people from the town have had four or five letters within this year—and I have not received one this twelve months—and I want to hear from home I shall write all oppertunities, and would have you do the same—
So No More at Presant
But I Remain Your Dutyfull Son till Death
                                        Samuell Searls

Source: Vakgroep Alfa-Informatica, Rijksuniversiteit Groningen, Department of Humanities Computing
http://grid.let.rug.nl/~usa/D/1776-1800/war

Summary:

We hear that most of the Parliament voted for America, so we should have peace by fall. We don't expect any fighting this year. Times are very hard. We aren't getting paid. But I hope the war will be over by fall. Please give my love to everyone and tell them I'll be home next fall if I'm alive, to see them and have a good time. We risk our lives, and they forget us. But soon they'll have to give us what's due. I find it hard that other people from there have had several letters this year, and I haven't had one. I'll write when I can, and hope you will too.

Vocabulary:
campaing = campaigning
venturing = risking
minde us = pay attention

Peace

In February of 1783, George III issued his Proclamation of Cessation of Hostilities, leading to the Peace Treaty of 1783. Signed in Paris on September 3, 1783, the agreement—also known as the Paris Peace Treaty—formally ended the United States War for Independence.

In addition to giving formal recognition to the U. S., the nine articles that embodied the treaty: established U. S. boundaries, specified certain fishing rights, allowed creditors of each country to be paid by citizens of the other, restored the rights and property of Loyalists, opened up the Mississippi River to citizens of both nations and provided for evacuation of all British forces.

Representing the United States were John Adams, Benjamin Franklin, and John Jay, all of whom signed the treaty.

Summary:

The King ackowledged that the 13 United States would be free and independent. He gave up all claims—both for himself and for his successors.

The treaty called for the end to any battles on sea or land, the release of prisoners, and the withdrawal of all Bristish forces from American soil. All American property, including Negroes, would remain in the United States.

Vocabulary:

Brittanic = British
sovereign = self-governing
relinquishes = gives up
propriety = proper, polite
successor = one that
  comes after
thereof = of that

Paris Peace Treaty – 1783

Article 1: His Brittanic Majesty acknowledges the said United States,...New Hampshire, Massachusetts Bay, Rhode Island and Providence Plantations, Connecticut, New York, New Jersey, Pennsylvania, Maryland, Virginia, North Carolina, South Carolina and Georgia,...to be free sovereign and independent...and for himself, his heirs, and successors, relinquishes all claims to the government, propriety, and territorial rights of the same and every part thereof.

Article 7: There shall be a firm and perpetual peace between his Brittanic Majesty and the said states,...wherefore all hostilities both by sea and land shall from henceforth cease. All prisoners on both sides shall be set at liberty, and his Brittanic Majesty shall with all convenient speed, and without causing any destruction, or carrying away any Negroes or other property of the American inhabitants, withdraw all his armies, garrisons, and fleets from the said United States....

Source: As it appears in *Jackson's Oxford Journal* England, October 4, 1783. Found on website: earlyamerica. com/earlyamerica/milestones/paris/text.html

Washington Portrait by Charles Wilson Peale

Washington Says Good-bye

In March, Washington had to talk his officers out of rebelling against the authority of Congress. In November, he retired from the army. Washington's farewell speech to the army praised the men highly—and also reminded them to become good members of society.

Washington's Farewell Orders issued to the Armies of the United States of America the 2d day of Novr 1783

It is earnestly recommended to all the Troops that…they should carry with them into civil Society the most conciliating dispositions; and that they should prove themselves not less virtuous and usefull as Citizens, than they have been persevering and victorious as Soldiers.

Source: University of Virginia, http://www.virginia.edu/ gwpapers

Summary:

It is sincerely suggested that the troops go into civilian life with good attitudes. They should be good citizens, just as they have been good soldiers.

Vocabulary:
civil = civilian
conciliating = soothing
dispositions = mood
earnestly = sincerely
persevereing = persistent

Afterword:
Learning to Run a Country
by Pat Perrin

Those who had fought for American independence now had their own country to run, and they had to learn how to do it. At that time, most governments were monarchies. To organize a country any other way was a new idea. There weren't many examples to follow.

In 1781, the 13 states developed their first constitution—the Articles of Confederation. They officially named themselves the United States of America. However, the states were far from being united. Each one considered itself independent. They did agree that a central government was needed for handling foreign policy. So each state sent representatives to a new Confederation Congress.

But the Congress had very little power. For example, Congress could request money from the states, but couldn't enforce payment. And any money it issued had little value. It soon became clear that this system wasn't going to work.

In 1786, Virginia and Maryland had a series of meetings to solve some problems between them. Those meetings grew into a larger convention, and eventually into a Constitutional Convention in Philadelphia in 1787.

The representatives to the Constitutional Convention had to start over. They decided to form a stronger central government. The 13 states were finally going to become one country.

The Revolutionary War had been fought with the belief that the American people could somehow govern themselves. Putting that belief into practice brought up ideas that hadn't been dealt with before. We're still trying to understand some of them.

For example, what do liberty and equality really mean? At that time, neither women nor slaves had equality with men who could hold property.

During the Revolutionary War, women had taken charge of farms and businesses. Some states recognized their economic importance. They changed a few laws to allow women to inherit property and to have some control over their economic affairs. However, most recognition of women still depended on their being mothers and wives.

Slaves who fought for the Patriots in the war were freed, and the northern states did away with slavery. But many, many people were still held as slaves in the South.

Americans were just beginning to learn what it meant to run their own country.

Research Activities/Things to Do

- Most Colonial women stayed at home during the war, caring for their families. What were the hardships and dangers they faced?

- Hessian troops were hired to fight for the British, when there were not enough British troops available to send to America. The wife of Hessian General von Riedesel went along with the troops, and her diary of the action gives us a fascinating report of what the soldiers faced in the days leading up to the Battle of Saratoga:

  Source: Jeanne Munn Bracken, ed., *Women in the American Revolution.* Carlisle, MA: Discovery Enterprises, Ltd., 1997, p. 35.

  ...Toward evening we finally reached Saratoga....The greatest misery and extreme disorder prevailed in the army The commissary had forgotten to distribute the food supplies among the troops; there were cattle enough, but not a single one had been slaughtered. More than thirty officers came to me because they could stand the hunger no longer. I had coffee and tea made for them and divided among them all the supplies with which my carriage was always filled; for we had a cook with us who, though an arch-rogue, nevertheless always knew how to get hold of something for us and, as we learned later, often crossed streams at night in order to steal from the farmers sheep, chickens, and pigs, which he sold to us at a good price....

- Women in the U.S. today may join the armed forces, but they are not permitted to fight on the front lines. Those whose husbands are in the military service may not accompany them to battle. After reading about women who participated in the Revolutionary War, do you think today's women should be allowed to fight or to go with their husbands? Explain your answer.

- In what way was Thomas Paine's *Common Sense* a turning point in the American Revolution?

- The November 27, 1775 letter of Abigail Adams to her husband John (noting the problems involved with establishing a new government for the colonies) has the following statement: "I am more and more convinced that man is a dangerous creature; and that power, whether vested in many or few, is ever grasping, and, like the grave, cries 'Give, Give.'" Explain.

Analyzing Cartoons Worksheet

Based on Worksheet from *Teaching with Documents,*
National Archives and Records Administration

1. **Describe the action taking place.**

2. **In your own words, explain the message.**

3. **List the key objects in the cartoon and describe what each symbolizes.**

   Object   *Symbolizes*

4. **How does the caption (if there is a caption) tie in with the picture?**

5. **If there are words in the illustration area of the cartoon, how do they enhance or relate to the caption?**

6. **What is the cartoonist's point of view?**

7. **Who do you think the intended audience is?**

8. **What is the significance of any dates or numbers that appear?**

9. **Are the people in the cartoon caricatures of famous people or just representative of average people or stereotypes of a group?**

Sample Cartoon

- This cartoon uses a famous scene from history to make a point about a big fight over school busing plans in Boston in the 1970s. What scene in history is shown here?

- The fight in Boston in the 1970s was over plans to bus children in order to get a more even balance of racial groups in the schools. Do you think this cartoon favors or opposes the school busing plan? Explain your answer.

Analyzing Songs/Poems Worksheet

1. **Type of song document:**
   ❑ Sheet music   ❑ Recording   ❑ Printed Lyrics only
   ❑ Other_____

2. **Time period from which the song or poem comes:**

3. **Date(s) on Song:**
   ❑ No Date   ❑ Copyright

4. **Composer:**   **Lyricist:**   **Poet:**

5. **For what audience was the piece written?**

6. **Key Information** (In your opinion, what is the message of the song/poem?)

7. **Do you think the song/poem was spontaneously written?**

8. **Choose a quote from the piece that helped you to know why it was written:**

9. **Write down two clues which you got from the words that tell you something about life in the U. S. at the time it was written:**

10. **What is the mood of the music or poetry?**

11. **Do you think the song/poem was used for propaganda? If so, describe the propaganda:**

12. **Does the wording have any "secret message" or symbolic meaning?**

Sample Song

"Songs...were an important element in the creation of the American nation, for they provided Americans with knowledge of a common tradition, a common literature, and a common morality. They gave a scattered and struggling people a sense of unity and common destiny amidst new and difficult problems.... There was a time for everything and a song for everything...."

Source: John Anthony Scott, *The Ballad of America-The History of the United States in Song and Story.* New York: Grosset & Dunlop Publishers, 1966, pp. 3, 6.

On October 19, 1781, British General Charles Cornwallis surrendered his entire army at Yorktown, ending the war. A broadside ballad describing this event was sung to a popular British marching song, "The British Grenadiers."

Source: Scott, *op. cit.*, verses 4 and 6, p 90.

Lord Cornwallis' Surrender

'Twas the nineteenth of October,
In the year of eighty-one,
Lord Cornwallis he surrendered
To General Washington.
They marched from their posts, brave boys,
And quickly grounded arms,
Rejoice you brave Americans,
With music's sweetest charms.

. . . .

Here's a health to great Washington,
And his brave army too
And likewise to our worthy Greene,
To him much honor's due.
May we subdue those English troops,
And clear the eastern shore,
That we may live in peace, my boys,
While wars they are no more.

- The fact that the 13 separate states had no joint source for obtaining money to cover the costs of war forced the Continental Congress to issue paper money or bills of credit. These bills were promises to pay the holders of them a certain sum of money in the future. Congress used them to buy supplies and to pay the soldiers. Each state was then supposed to give money to Congress so it could give silver or gold to the owners of the bills. But this was not done, and no cash fund was created to keep up their value. The new currency was as good as worthless. Do some research to find out about the history of the U. S. Treasury and how money actually came to be worth something after the war. (Start at http://odur.let.rug.nl/~usa/E/usbank/bank03.html)

Source: *The American Revolution—A Picturebook*, p. 146.

- Americans knew the lay of the land and where the fighting had to be done better than the British did. They were used to the rough living conditions which war brought. The typical settler felt quite at home with a rifle in hand. After doing some further reading on the battles in the war, compare some of the tactics of the Patriots and the British.

- The damage done by the redcoats angered the people and aroused their fighting spirit. Britain's soldiers had no real interest in the war, while the Americans were defending their firesides and their settled way of life. Having to bring troops and supplies across the ocean made England's task all the greater. Describe ways in which the spirit of the Patriots inspired them to win the war.

John Paul Jones, encouraging his men to attack. (Drawing by Darley)

John Paul Jones was given command of an old French merchant ship, which he rebuilt and named the *Bon Homme Richard ("Poor Richard")* to honor Benjamin Franklin. He set out with a small fleet and, on Sept. 23, 1779, he encountered the British frigate *Serapis* and a smaller warship. Despite the superiority of the *Serapis*, Jones did not hesitate to engage it in battle.

The battle, which began at sunset and ended more than three and a half hours later by moonlight, was one of the most memorable in naval history. Jones sailed close in, to cut the advantage of the *Serapis*, and finally in the battle lashed the *Bon Homme Richard* to the British ship. Both ships were heavily damaged. The *Serapis* was on fire in at least 12 places. The hull of the *Bon Homme Richard* was pierced, her decks were ripped, her hold was filling with water, and fires were destroying her; yet when the British captain asked if Jones was ready to surrender, he proudly answered, "Sir, I have not yet begun to fight." When the *Serapis* surrendered, Jones and his men boarded her while his own ship sank.

• Write a poem or a song about John Paul Jones' part in the war. You may want to do some more research before you begin.

Suggested Further Reading

Companion Literature Compiled by Ellin Rossberg

The books listed below are suggested readings in American literature, which tie in with the *Researching American History Series*. The selections were made based on feedback from teachers and librarians currently using them in interdisciplinary classes for students in grades 5 to 12. Of course there are many other historical novels that would be appropriate to tie in with the titles in this series.

The American Revolution

Johnny Tremain, Esther Forbes - EL/M

Fighting Ground, Avi - EL

The Bells of Freedom, Dorothy Gilman - M

Early Thunder, Jean Fritz - M

War Comes to Willie Freeman, James Lincoln Collier & Christopher Collier - M

Enemy Among Them, Deborah H. DeFord & Harry S. Stout - M

My Brother Sam is Dead, James Lincoln Collier & Christopher Collier - M

Guns for General Washington, Seymour Reit - M

Fifth of March: A Story of the Boston Massacre, Ann Rinaldi - M

Toliver's Secret, Esther Wood Brady - M

The Bloody Country, James Lincoln Collier and Christopher Collier - M

Sarah Bishop, Scott O'Dell - M

April Morning, Harvard Fast - M

Benjamin Franklin: The Autobiography and Other Writings, Benjamin Franklin - HS

Journal of William Thomas Emerson, Revolutionary War Patriot, Barry Denenberg - EL

The French and Indian War

I Am Regina, Sally M. Keehn - M

*Last of the Mohicans * Deerslayer * The Pathfinder * The Leatherstocking Tales,* James Fenimore Cooper - HS

Northwest Passage, Kenneth Roberts - HS

For information on these and other titles from Discovery Enterprises, Ltd., call or write to: Discovery Enterprises, Ltd., 31 Laurelwood Drive, Carlisle, MA 01741 Phone: 978-287-5401 Fax: 978-287-5402